Keeping Tadpoles (Alive!)

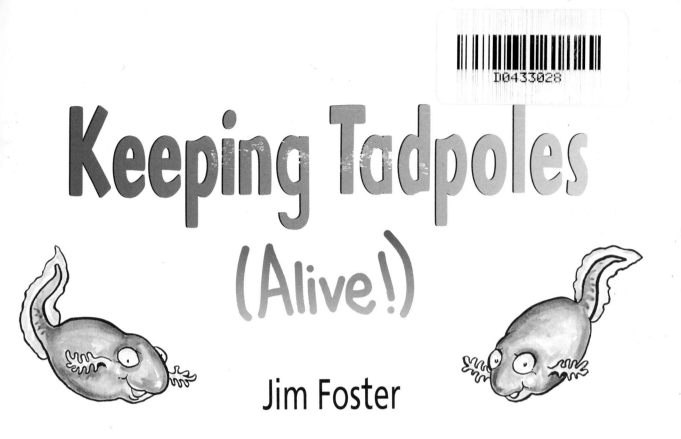

Jim Foster

on behalf of

FROG*life*

Acknowledgements

Photos
Bruce Coleman Ltd/Jane Burton, cover, page 10 bottom, page 12 middle left and middle right, page 18 top. Bruce Coleman Ltd/Andy Purcell, page 7 bottom. NHPA/Martin Wendler, page 11 top. Oxford Scientific Films/G. I. Bernard, page 11 bottom, page 13 top, page 15 top left and right, page 16 middle right and bottom, page 17 middle, page 19 middle right, page 21 top. Bruce Coleman Ltd/Kim Taylor, page 12 top right. London Scientific Films/Oxford Scientific Films, page 14 top. NHPA/Stephen Dalton, page 16 middle left. NHPA/G. I. Bernard, page 19 middle left. Heather Angel, page 22 top.

For further information on keeping tadpoles, please contact Froglife, Triton House, Bramfield, Halesworth, Suffolk IP19 9AE. Tel: 01986 784518. Fax: 01986 784579. Froglife is a non profit-making organisation which provides information on amphibian and reptile conservation in garden and countryside environments.

Designed by Jim Evoy

Illustrations
All illustrations by Oxford Illustrators

The week numbers given in this book are for guidance only. Some tadpoles develop faster than others. Temperature and food quality can affect how fast tadpoles grow.

Heinemann Educational Publishers
Halley Court, Jordan Hill, Oxford OX2 8EJ
a division of Reed Educational & Professional Publishing Ltd

OXFORD   MELBOURNE   AUCKLAND
JOHANNESBURG   BLANTYRE   GABORONE
IBADAN   PORTSMOUTH (NH) USA   CHICAGO

© Reed Educational & Professional Publishing Ltd 1997

First published 1997

02 01 00 99

10 9 8 7 6 5

British Library Cataloguing in Publication Data
A catalogue record for this book is available from the British Library.

ISBN 0 435 09566 8   *Keeping Tadpoles (Alive!)* individual copy pack:
                                6 copies of 1 title

ISBN 0 435 09416 5   Stage F pack: 1 each of 7 titles

Colour reproduction by Reacta Graphics.

Printed and bound in Great Britain by Scotprint.

Contents

Introduction

Keeping tadpoles can be exciting.
In this book you will find out

- how to collect tadpoles

- how to look after your tadpoles
  and keep them alive

- what to do with your tadpoles
  when they have fully grown

Things to remember

- ask the pond owner for permission
  before taking frogspawn

- cover cuts on your hands with
  waterproof plasters

- do not eat food while visiting
  the pond

- always wash your hands after
  visiting the pond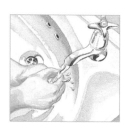

What you will need

You will need

- one small net and one large, strong net

- a glass or plastic aquarium

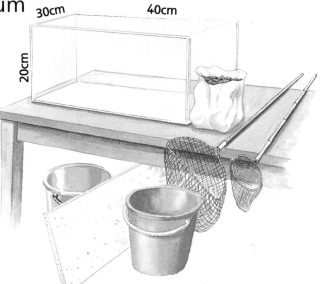

- a sheet of polystyrene

- two clean buckets

- rabbit food pellets

30cm   40cm   20cm

Put the aquarium on top of the polystyrene. Put the aquarium in a place where it will get some sunlight. Tadpoles grow faster in warm water.

Do not give your tadpoles too much direct sunlight.

Preparing your aquarium

Use the buckets to put water into the aquarium. Leave the water to 'breathe' for two days before putting in your tadpoles. Fresh tap water is harmful to tadpoles.

Keep two buckets of tap water ready to use for changing the water.

Finding frogspawn

Tadpoles start life as eggs. Adult frogs lay eggs in the spring. The eggs are called frogspawn.

Frogspawn can be found at the edge of a pond. It looks like a lump of clear jelly. The jelly contains lots of small, black eggs.

Ponds

Go to a pond with an adult or teacher. Ask the pond owner for permission before taking any frogspawn. Do not stand in the pond. You will see the frogs and their spawn from the edge.

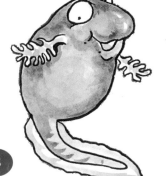

Collect frogspawn from a pond in a park or garden near your school. Do not disturb wild ponds in the countryside.

Collecting frogspawn

To collect your frogspawn you will need

- the large, strong net

- a clean bucket

Fill the bucket half full with pond water. Gently lift a small clump of frogspawn from the pond with the net. Put the frogspawn in the bucket with a small piece of pond weed. Take the bucket to the aquarium straight away.

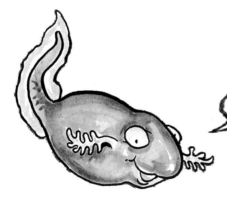

Carry the bucket as still as possible.

Day 1

Put the frogspawn into the aquarium using the net. Do not worry if it sinks to the bottom. Put the pond weed into the aquarium.

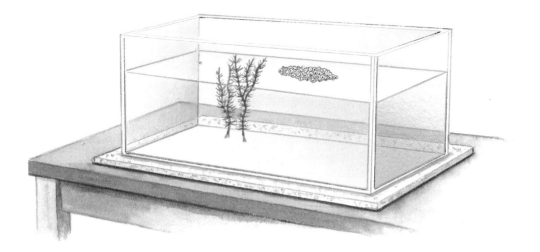

There may be more than 1,000 tiny black eggs in one lump of frogspawn.

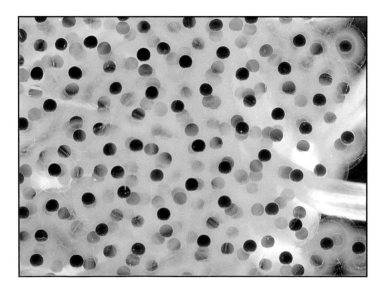

Week 1

Do not put any food into the aquarium. The eggs are still surrounded by jelly.

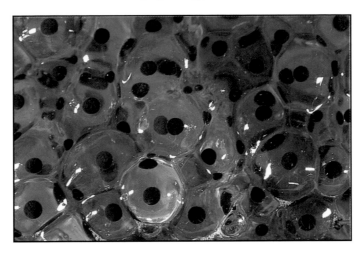

The frogspawn will soon swell up as the jelly absorbs water.

The time it takes your frogspawn to hatch out will depend on when it was laid.

Week 2

Development

The eggs change shape. They get longer. After a few days they develop small tails. The eggs are now called embryos.

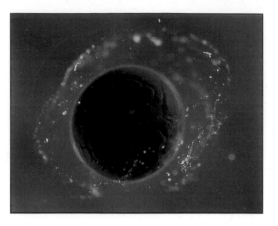

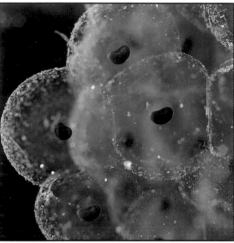

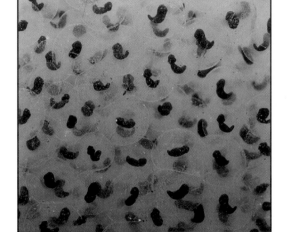

Feeding and care

The water in the aquarium may start to smell or look cloudy. Take some of the water out. Replace it with some water from one of the buckets. Do not touch the eggs.

Week 3

Development

The embryos start to hatch. They are now called tadpoles.

Feeding and care

Half fill a clean bucket with some of the water you have left to breathe. Keep 30 of the tadpoles in the aquarium to study. Collect the rest in a net and put them in the bucket. Take them back to the pond where you collected the frogspawn. Gently put them into the pond.

Always return tadpoles to the pond where you collected the frogspawn.

Week 3

Development

The tadpoles will grow gills. The gills help the tadpoles to breathe. The tadpoles also have special teeth.

Feeding and care

When the tadpoles leave the jelly, they will need food. Put three rabbit pellets (each about 1cm long) into the aquarium. The tadpoles will also eat algae growing on the pond weed.

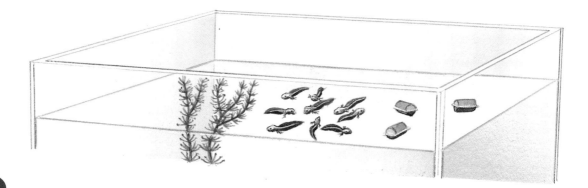

Week 4

Development

The shape of the tadpoles changes. Their tails get longer. Their gills get smaller.

Feeding and care

Carefully change the water in the aquarium if it becomes dirty. If the tadpoles eat all the pellets, add some more.

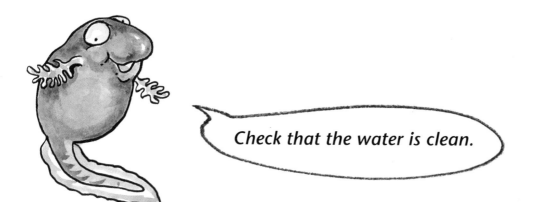

Check that the water is clean.

Weeks 5–6

Development

The back legs of the tadpoles start to grow. They grow where the tail joins the body. The legs are very small, but grow quickly.

Feeding and care

Start to give the tadpoles a little more food. Give them six pellets every three days.

Weeks 7–10

Development

The tadpoles start to develop toes on their
back legs. They use their tails to move around.
The tail has a line of muscles down its middle.

Feeding and care

Any uneaten food in the water is harmful. Change
the water and food regularly.

*Clean water in the aquarium is
very important now.*

Weeks 11–12

Development

The tadpoles now have very wide mouths. One front leg starts to grow. Then the other front leg grows.

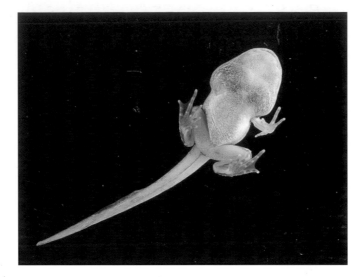

Feeding and care

Carefully take out two thirds of the water from the aquarium. Put a rock in the water. Make sure that part of it is above the water. Put some damp moss on the top of the rock. Float a piece of cork on the water.

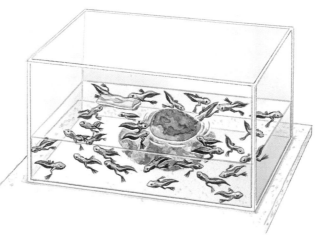

Weeks 11–12

Development

When the tadpoles have their front legs, they come out of the water. Their gills have disappeared. The tadpoles have lungs inside their bodies. Their bodies get flatter. Their tails start to shrink. They are now called froglets.

Feeding and care

When the tadpoles have two front legs, do not add any food. Tadpoles do not eat food for a few days now.

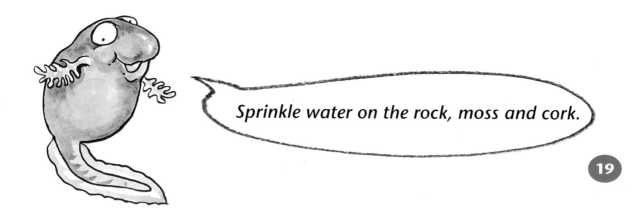

Sprinkle water on the rock, moss and cork.

Froglets

Development

When the froglets have all four legs, they should be returned to their natural surroundings. You may need to take some froglets back every day. It may take a few weeks before all the froglets have four legs.

Returning the froglets

Line a bucket with damp grass. Wet your hands and carefully pick the froglets out of the aquarium. Put them in the bucket. Take the froglets back to the pond where you collected them. Gently pick up each froglet. Put it down in some long grass, next to the pond.

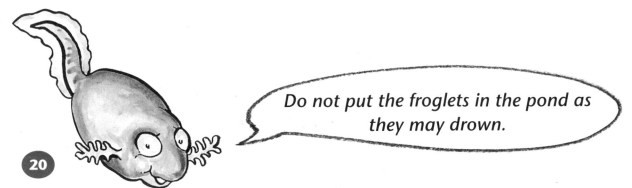

Do not put the froglets in the pond as they may drown.

Visiting the froglets

Throughout the summer and autumn, go back to the pond and look at your froglets. Their tails are absorbed into their bodies. The froglets then start to feed on tiny animals such as flies. They grow much bigger.

When winter comes, the froglets find a place to hibernate under rocks or logs.

The froglets grow much bigger when they start to feed on tiny animals.

Adult frogs

The froglets have now become young frogs. The young frogs will live on land for two or three years. They then become adult frogs and will return to a pond to breed. They will probably return to the same pond where you first saw the frogspawn!

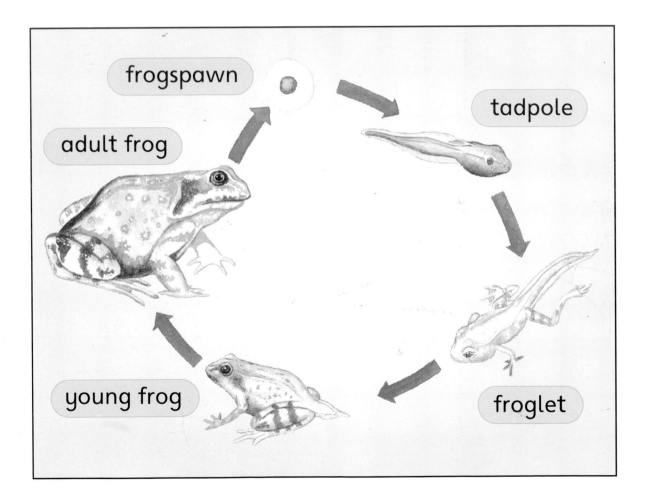

frogspawn

tadpole

adult frog

froglet

young frog

New homes

Many ponds are destroyed when new roads and houses are built. If a pond is destroyed, the frogs that live there will be homeless. Some of the frogs will not survive.

You can build a new pond at your school, or in a garden. Your pond will give frogs and other wildlife a new home.

Index

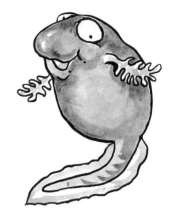